TABLE OF CONTENTS

INTRODUCTION

Honor. Courage. Commitment. These are the values of a United States Marine. Every thought and every action must be guided by these values. A Marine's strength must be unmatched. Each Marine has a responsibility to those that came before and those that will come after. The future is theirs to lead.

Marines have been some of the first troops in and the last to leave since 1775. The U.S. Marine Corps began as a part of the U.S. Navy. The first Marine mission was a raid on Fort Nassau in The Bahamas during the American Revolutionary War (1775–1783). The Marines became their own military branch in 1798. Since then, they have been serving and protecting America at home and around the world.

Today, the U.S. Marine Corps has about 172,000 **active duty** members. These Marines serve as intelligence experts, translators, and lawyers. They serve as security advisors, engineers, and more! The Marine Corps includes more than 300 different careers that make the Corps what it is.

Over the years, many have served. Many have died. All should be honored.

"THE MARINES' HYMN"

The song "The Marines' Hymn" is the official hymn of the U.S. Marine Corps. The song can be traced to the 1860s. The music is from an opera called Genevieve de Brabant written by Jacques Offenbach. But no one knows who wrote the words. It's still a mystery.

From the Halls of Montezuma
To the shores of Tripoli;

"Our hymn has immense meaning to us because it is based on our history. We are who we are because of our brothers and sisters who have gone before us. We desire to never let them down."

–SE Nelson, Veteran Marine, 2025

We fight our country's battles

LOOK

Look at this historical image of Marines. How do they look different from modern Marines you see in this book?

★ **MARINE CORPS FACTS** The Battle of Belleau Wood in World War I (1914–1918) gave the Marines another nickname. U.S. Marines helped the French win the battle. They didn't give up. It earned them the nickname "Devil Dogs."

In the air, on land, and sea;

★ **MARINE CORPS FACTS** "The Marines' Hymn" was revised in 1942 during World War II (1939–1945). The line "On the land as on the sea" was changed to "In the air, on land, and sea." Marine pilots had just provided vital air support at the Battle of Guadalcanal.

First to fight for right and freedom
And to keep our honor clean;

★ **MARINE CORPS FACTS** The Navajo Code Talkers were a special Marine force. They fought in World War II. They used the Navajo language to communicate battle plans. The Japanese couldn't break the code. No one knew about it until the program was **declassified** in 1968.

We are proud to claim the title

ASK QUESTIONS

Why do you think the Marines chose a Latin motto? Do some digging to find the answer.

★ **MARINE CORPS FACTS** The **motto** of the U.S. Marines is *Semper Fidelis*. It means "always faithful" in Latin. Marines are loyal to their fellow Marines. They are committed to fighting for their country. Their battle cry is "Oorah." It is part of Marine tradition. It unites them.

Of United States Marine!

★ **MARINE CORPS FACTS** The name "Marine" comes from French. The word *marine* in French means "navy" in English. It makes sense for this fighting force. The Marines started as the **ground troops** of the U.S. Navy. They grew to be much more.

Our flag's unfurled to every breeze From dawn to setting sun;

★ **MARINE CORPS FACTS** A famous photo shows Marines raising a U.S. flag during the Battle of Iwo Jima in World War II. The United States won this battle. A statue in Arlington, Virginia, recreates this photograph. It honors Marines who gave their lives to fight for their country.

We have fought in every clime and place
Where we could take a gun;

★ **MARINE CORPS FACTS** The U.S. Marines travel to places all around the world to fight for the United States. They have been fighting for America since 1775. When the country calls, Marines respond.

In the snow of far-off Northern lands
And in sunny tropic scenes,

MAKE A GUESS

Is there anywhere in the world you think the Marines haven't gone? Make a guess! Then research to find out if you're right.

"I have just returned from visiting the Marines at the front, and there is not a finer fighting organization in the world."

— General Douglas MacArthur, Seoul, Korea, September 21, 1950

You will find us always on the job

★ **MARINE CORPS FACTS** The Marines help during **natural disasters**. They help survivors **evacuate**. Operation Sea Angel took place in 1991. It was the largest military relief effort ever. 400 Marines took part. They delivered food, water, and medical care. They saved lives.

The United States Marines!

★ **MARINE CORPS FACTS** Lieutenant General Lewis Burwell "Chesty" Puller (1898–1971) became the most decorated Marine in history. He served for 37 years and earned 14 individual awards. They include five Navy Crosses for **heroism** in combat.

Here's health to you and to our Corps
Which we are proud to serve;

THINK

Why do you think it's important for Marines to move from water to land quickly?

★ **MARINE CORPS FACTS** Marines are known for their amphibious vehicles. These vehicles can travel from water to land. The Assault Amphibious Vehicle (AAV) has been used since 1972. It is being replaced by the Amphibious Combat Vehicle (ACV).

In many a strife we've fought for life
And never lost our nerve.

★ **MARINE CORPS FACTS** Millions of people are Marine Corps **veterans**. Of all U.S. military veterans, about 11 percent served in the Marine Corps. The Marine Corps has a saying, "Once a Marine, always a Marine." Those that served are Marines for life.

If the Army and the Navy
Ever look on Heaven's scenes,

★ **MARINE CORPS FACTS** The Marine Corps has 21 active bases and air stations. The United States is home to 19 of them. California and North Carolina have the most. There are five Marine bases in California. There are four in North Carolina. There are also two in Japan.

"I'm constantly humbled by the quality and dedication of the . . . Americans who continue to measure themselves against our high standards [and] who compete for the title of Marine: Earned, never given."

– Commandant of the Marine Corps General Eric M. Smith, 2025

They will find the streets are guarded By United States Marines!

CREATE

Make a video of friends and neighbors saying, "Thank you for your service." Create a poster that says, "THANK YOU, MARINES!" Ask a trusted adult to help you share these with Marines and veteran Marines in your community.

from the RIFLEMAN'S CREED

This is my rifle. There are many like it, but this one is mine.

My rifle is my best friend. It is my life. I must
master it as I must master my life.

My rifle is human, even as I, because it is my life. Thus,
I will learn it as a brother. I will learn its weaknesses, its
strength, its parts, its accessories, its sights and its barrel.

Before God, I swear this creed. My rifle and myself
are the defenders of my country. We are the masters
of our enemy. We are the saviors of my life.

So be it, until victory is America's and
there is no enemy, but peace!

LEARN MORE

BOOKS

Coupé, Jessica. *US Marine Corps*. Mendota Heights, MN: Apex Editions, 2023.

Gagne, Tammy. *The Armed Forces Encyclopedia*. Minneapolis, MN: ABDOPublishing, 2024.

Hamilton, John. *United States Marine Corps*. Minneapolis, MN: ABDO Publishing, 2021.

WEBSITES

Search these online sources with an adult.

Marines' Hymn facts for kids | Kiddle

The Marines' Hymn (lyrics) | USMC hymn | JR videos | video

GLOSSARY

active duty (AK-tiv-DOO-tee) describing a member of the U.S. Armed Forces who works for the military full-time and can be deployed

Amphibious Combat Vehicle (am-FIH-bee-uhs KAHM-bat VEE-uh-kuhl) armored vehicle designed to transport troops from sea to shore; ACVs can float on water and drive on land

declassified (dee-KLA-suh-fied) removed security clearance for; made public

evacuate (ih-VA-kyuh-wayt) remove from a dangerous area

ground troops (GROWND TROOPS) armed forces who fight on land

heroism (HAIR-uh-wih-zuhm) great bravery

intel (IN-tel) useful information about a subject of interest

motto (MAH-toh) short expression or guiding principle

natural disasters (NACH-uh-ruhl dih-ZAS-terz) sudden events in nature causing serious damage, death, or injury

veterans (VEH-tuh-ruhnz) former members of the armed forces

INDEX